BLESSED IS THE MATCH

THE LIFE AND DEATH OF HANNAH SENESH

A **FACING HISTORY AND OURSELVES** STUDY GUIDE

FACING
HISTORY
AND
OURSELVES

Facing History and Ourselves is an international educational and professional development organization whose mission is to engage students of diverse backgrounds in an examination of racism, prejudice, and antisemitism in order to promote the development of a more humane and informed citizenry. By studying the historical development of the Holocaust and other examples of genocide, students make the essential connection between history and the moral choices they confront in their own lives. For more information about Facing History, please visit our website at www.facinghistory.org.

Copyright © 2008 by Katahdin Foundation and Facing History and Ourselves. All rights reserved.

Facing History and Ourselves® is a trademark registered in the U.S. Patent & Trademark Office.

Poems and photos courtesy of the Hannah Senesh Legacy Foundation www.hannahsenesh.org.il

To receive additional copies of this resource, please visit www.facinghistory.org/publications.

ISBN-13: 978-0-9798440-6-5
ISBN-10: 0-9798440-6-1

FACING HISTORY AND OURSELVES

Facing History and Ourselves Headquarters
16 Hurd Road
Brookline, MA 02445-6919

ACKNOWLEDGMENTS

Facing History and Ourselves expresses much gratitude to Katahdin Productions and the Monica and Phil Rosenthal Family Trust for providing the support to make this study guide possible.

We also extend a special thank you to the Senesh family for their significant contributions to the study guide, along with granting Facing History and Ourselves permission to use key materials.

There a number of Facing History and Ourselves' staff members who deserve recognition: Leora Schaefer wrote the study guide. Adam Strom, Marc Skvirsky, and Jan Darsa made numerous, thoughtful contributions to the text. Jenifer Snow designed the study guide, and Catherine O'Keefe managed the publishing components. Finally, Nicole Breaux managed the project.

TABLE OF CONTENTS

Introduction vi

Message from the Film Director vii

Message from the Senesh Family ix

Section One: Preview 10
    Background Information 12
    Hannah Senesh 12
    HISTORICAL TIMELINE 14
    Classroom Strategies 19

Section Two: Postview 22
    Classroom Strategies 22
    Handout One: Poetry by Hannah Senesh 27
    Handout Two: Rescue and Responsibility 28

About the Partnership 29

INTRODUCTION

This study guide has been developed to accompany the film *Blessed Is the Match: The Life and Death of Hannah Senesh*. The guide is organized in two sections: Preview and Postview. In the Preview, students are introduced to Hannah Senesh. They learn the historical context of her story, and they begin to consider some of the main themes of the film. In the Postview, students will deepen their understanding of the main themes through a close examination of excerpts from Senesh's diary and letters, as well as her poetry. Each section of the guide includes classroom strategies and activities that will support students as they consider the significance of Senesh's life and the legacy that she leaves for young people today.

This guide is intended to act as a menu of ideas for how to incorporate *Blessed Is the Match* into a middle or high school course. It provides suggested activities that can be chosen according to the focus subject area, age of students, and amount of time that can be allotted to the film. We recommend that at least one class session be dedicated to the preview activities, then one session to watch the film, leaving at least one session for postview activities and debrief.

Throughout this guide you will see references to feature-length and classroom-cut versions of the film. The classroom version is 45 minutes long and has been edited so that it can be viewed in one class session. The feature-length film is 90 minutes and, as such, goes deeper into the story of Senesh's life. This study guide has been designed for use in classrooms where either version of the film has been seen.

THE FACING HISTORY AND OURSELVES JOURNAL

Throughout this study guide, students are asked to record their thoughts in journals. In most Facing History and Ourselves classrooms, teachers and students reflect on their learning by keeping journals. These serve multiple purposes in a Facing History classroom. Using journals with students can help them accomplish the following:

–Reflect on the lesson and the questions raised about responsibility to themselves and others
–Develop writing skills
–Connect content to students' personal experiences
–Formulate their own opinions before the class discussion
–Document how their thinking changes over time

MESSAGE FROM THE FILM DIRECTOR

My film *Blessed Is the Match: The Life and Death of Hannah Senesh* is the first feature-length documentary about Hannah Senesh. To tell Hannah's story is a lifelong dream come true, an honor, and a daunting responsibility. Despite Hannah's status as a national heroine in Israel, her story is little known in the rest of the world, but I hope that my film will help to change that.

I first read Hannah's diary in junior high school and was captivated by her courage and touched by her vulnerability. Later, as a history student in college, where I wrote my senior thesis on the Nazi SS, Hannah's story continued to inspire me. Why? She fought back. In the face of monolithic evil, she chose to act by joining a noble, against-all-odds mission.

For the past 20 years, as I've worked as a documentary filmmaker, my interest in Hannah has persisted. But my fascination with her story has come to include her mother's experience as well. This is not just because I've grown from a student Hannah's age to a mother closer to Catherine's age (although, admittedly, that could be part of it). It is also because in many ways Catherine is a figure we can understand better than we can Hannah.

Hannah is a modern-day Joan of Arc, the type of heroine who comes along once in a century—bold, brilliant, and uncommonly courageous. Catherine, however, represents us all. As a worried mother, she watches her child drift away, pursue her own path, and then make the ultimate sacrifice—as only the young can do. Worst of all, Catherine must have spent the remainder of her days wondering if Hannah's motivation was to save the Jews of Hungary or simply to save her mother.

In 2005 the Senesh family granted us the rights to Hannah's life story and unprecedented access to the Senesh family archives. In this rich archive—in addition to Hannah's diary—are hundreds of unpublished letters and nearly 1,300 never-before-seen photos of remarkable quality, more than half taken by Hannah herself. She had meticulously recorded her life not just in words but also in pictures. Access to this archive was just the beginning of the critical input of the Senesh family in the making of the film. For the three years of production, Eitan Senesh, the son of Hannah's brother Giora, worked tirelessly to ensure accuracy in the film. Eitan, who along with his brother David lives in Israel, oversaw the cataloging of family photographs, the translation of letters, and the search for people who knew Hannah. He attended all the shoots and commented on scripts and edits of the film.

In 2006 and 2007 we shot the film in Hungary, Israel, and the Czech Republic. Our interview subjects included scholars and survivors, witnesses and friends of Hannah's from Budapest and Palestine. We gained new insight into the parachutists' mission from the two surviving parachutists—Surika Braverman and Reuven Dafni, shortly before Reuven's death. Perhaps the most chilling interviews were conducted with four women who were in the same Gestapo prison as Catherine and Hannah Senesh in 1944.

Making *Blessed Is the Match* has been a long and complex journey. We hope our film does justice to Hannah's story, to her character, to her creativity, and to her courage. We also hope it tells a moving and multilayered mother-daughter story. By doing this, we hope to honor the legacies of both Hannah and Catherine Senesh for years to come.

Roberta Grossman
Director, *Blessed Is the Match: The Life and Death of Hannah Senesh*

MESSAGE FROM THE SENESH FAMILY

Although I didn't know my late aunt Hannah Senesh, her story has accompanied me for my entire life. Because of her heroism, the name "Senesh" has taken on great meaning in the small nation of Israel, and it wasn't always easy growing up with this name. Over the years, I have also come to view my aunt's life story differently—as not merely an affirming heroic story, but as a more complicated and interesting human story. Since Hannah's execution more than 60 years ago, countless books and articles have been written about her and many documentaries and feature films have been made. But none have captured the human side of Hannah—of a talented, creative, and sensitive young woman who was determined to achieve her goals, adhere to her moral values, and contribute to her society without asking for anything in return. I believe the meaning and messages of Hannah's life are both unique and universal. My deeper understanding of my aunt's life has led me to want to share more of her story with the public—especially with young people.

After my father Giora passed away, I took over the responsibility of managing Hannah's family archive. My main goal has been to change Hannah's image from an abstract, mythical heroine to real young woman. I have tried to do this by publishing more of her letters, diary entries, and poetry (included in a new English edition of Hannah's diary), and by emphasizing unknown parts of her life story. This is reflected in educational activities supported by the "Hannah Senesh Legacy Foundation" at Beit Hannah at Kibbutz Sdot-Yam in Israel. Most recently, the "Hannah Senesh Legacy Foundation" has been working to translate Hannah's writings from Hungarian to Hebrew and English.

With the documentary film, *Blessed Is the Match*, director Roberta Grossman has given us the means to make Hannah's story better known throughout the world. The film introduces Hannah to viewers and offers a portrait of someone we can relate to. I hope the film fulfills its educational aims and can be used as a tool for educating young viewers and future generations about the values of honoring people and contributing to society. As you are watching it, reading Hannah's poetry, or leading discussions about Hannah, I hope you might ask yourself: "What can I do for others?" "What are my goals and how can I achieve them?" and "What lessons can I learn from Hannah's life story?" I hope you'll ask these questions not because you've been inspired by a mythical figure, but instead by a gifted and very human young woman who was able to light the way for those around her. As Hannah wrote: "There are stars whose radiance is visible on earth though they have long been extinct. There are people whose brilliance continues to light the world though they are no longer among the living. These lights are particularly bright when the night is dark. They light the way for mankind."

Eitan Senesh, Hannah Senesh's nephew
Hannah Senesh Legacy Foundation

Preview

This section of the study guide provides teaching strategies as well as background information that will help prepare your students to view *Blessed Is the Match: The Life and Death of Hannah Senesh*. The background information can be helpful in providing you, as the classroom teacher, information to share with your students. Alternatively, you can print out this section and have your students read it on their own or in groups.

BACKGROUND INFORMATION

Jewish Life in Hungary Before World War II

In 1867 Jews living in Hungary were given full emancipation and were permitted to participate in all aspects of Hungarian life as citizens. By 1869 the Jewish population of Hungary had reached 542,000 from 12,000 only 100 years earlier.

Although the Jewish community of Hungary benefited from participation in all aspects of Hungarian society, a rise of antisemitism impacted the daily lives of Jews. State-sponsored anti-Jewish propaganda was prevalent in the 1870s and 1880s. However, even with this rise in antisemitism, by 1910 the Jewish population of Hungary had risen to 910,000 (5 percent of the total population).

In the years leading up to World War I, the Jewish community of Hungary contained a broad spectrum of religious affiliation. Many Jews were assimilated and secular. Others were observant of the Jewish tradition. Centers of Jewish learning developed in parts of the country, including a famous and well-respected yeshiva (place of Jewish learning) in Pressburg.

During these years, Jewish citizens were members of professional groups, such as medicine or law. They also participated in business and the arts. Many Jews enlisted and fought in World War I. Ten thousand Hungarian Jews died in that war.

After World War I Hungary was led by a short-lived communist regime until June 1919 when the country came under the control of Admiral Miklos Horthy. Horthy, a self-described antisemite, declared himself Regent of Hungary and began revoking the rights of Hungarian Jews in 1920 when a law was passed that restricted the number of Jews who could be accepted to institutes of higher learning.

Hungary and the Holocaust

In November 1940 Hungary joined the Axis alliance, siding with Germany in the war. This decision was partly influenced by Hungary's nationalist and fascist entities, which in turn were heavily influenced by the Nazi movement. Hungary also hoped to acquire additional land as Germany began to redraw national borders in Europe.

Between 1938 and 1941 Hungary began instituting anti-Jewish legislation based on the Nazi's Nuremberg Laws. Jews became defined by racial terms; rights that had been afforded to Hungarian Jews in 1867 were revoked. In addition, Jews and non-Jews were not allowed to intermarry; Jews were excluded from certain professions; and Jews were restricted from participating in economic life. Life for Hungarian Jews under Miklos Horthy was difficult. However, even under pressure from the Nazis in 1942 to begin to deport the Jews, Hungarian Prime Minister Miklos Kallay (appointed by Horthy on March 9, 1942) refused to do so.

After the Germans were defeated in Stalingrad in 1943, the defeat of the Nazis seemed likely. Kallay began secret negotiations to join the Allied powers. The Germans invaded Hungary on March 19, 1944, having learned about Kallay's talks with the West, and being angered by the lack of Hungarian participation in the war and its refusal to deport Hungary's Jews. The Nazis replaced Kallay with General Dome Sztojay, who had previously served as Hungarian minister to Berlin and was fanatically pro-German, as prime minister.

The Hungarian Jews were the last to be deported by the Nazis. By April 1944 Jewish communities outside Budapest were ghettoized, and by May Jews were rounded up and deported to concentration camps, primarily to Auschwitz. In 1941, Jews numbering 825,000 were living in Hungary. By July 1944 nearly 440,000 Jews had been deported, and the only Jewish community that remained in Hungary was in Budapest.

Horthy, fearing German defeat and being implicated in war crimes, on July 7 called a halt to all of the deportations. He dismissed the Sztojay government and tried to establish peace with the Soviet Union. In response the Germans sponsored a coup d'etat and arrested Horthy. They installed a new Hungarian government under Ferenc Szalasi, the leader of the fascist and radically antisemitic Arrow Cross Party.

The Arrow Cross Party carried out the murder of the Jews of Budapest. Thousands of Jews were executed and thrown into the Danube River in Budapest. In November the remaining Jewish community was ghettoized and thousands of Jews were sent on a death march to the border of Austria.

By April 1945 all of Hungary had been liberated by the Soviet Union. Five hundred and sixty thousand Hungarian Jews were murdered during the Holocaust.

Sources:
Randolf L. Braham, *The Politics of Genocide* (New York: Columbia University Press, 1981).

Randolf L. Braham and Scott Miller, *The Nazis' Last Victims: The Holocaust in Hungary* (Detroit: Wayne State University Press, 1998).

United States Holocaust Memorial Museum, "Holocaust Encyclopedia," *http://www.ushmm.org/wlc/en/*

HANNAH SENESH

Hannah Senesh was born in Budapest, Hungary, on July 17, 1921, into a prominent and acculturated Jewish family. Her father, Bela Senesh, was a famous journalist and playwright who had eight plays produced in Budapest before his death at age 33. Hannah was only six years old when her father died; her brother Giora was seven. Growing up, Hannah had a very close relationship with her mother Catherine, her brother, and her grandmother, who lived with the family until she died in 1937. Hannah began writing in a diary at the age of 13.

As a teenager, Hannah attended a prestigious Protestant girls' school in Budapest, which Jewish students were permitted to attend. However, as Jews, they had to pay triple the tuition the other students paid. Nevertheless, Hannah excelled in school and in other extracurricular activities. She tutored her classmates, became an accomplished photographer, and dreamed of following in her father's footsteps by becoming a writer. She enjoyed a culturally rich life filled with classical music concerts, plays, books, sports, and travel throughout Hungary and Europe.

In 1937, Hannah was nominated to be an officer in her high school's Literary Society, but a new election was called so that a Jewish student would not take office. During this period, Hannah began learning about Zionism. (Historically this was a political and social movement that supported the establishment of a Jewish homeland in Palestine—modern-day Israel). Hannah began to learn Hebrew (the language of Jews living in Palestine), and to participate in the Zionist youth movement in Hungary.

In 1938, Hannah's brother Giora graduated from high school, but was unable to attend university because of restrictions on the number of Jewish students. Hannah's mother Catherine decided that Giora should go to France to study textiles.

Hannah Senesh writing at her desk, 1936.

Giora's departure and the rising antisemitism in Hungary profoundly affected Hannah. In 1939, at age 18, she decided to move to Palestine to study at the Nahalal Agricultural School for Girls. Catherine opposed her daughter's plans to emigrate to Palestine. She was particularly unhappy about Hannah's decision to study agriculture, instead of pursuing an intellectual career in the university. Hannah could not be swayed: "There are already far too many intellectuals in Palestine. The need is for workers to help build up the country."[1]

Hannah left Hungary for Palestine in September 1939 and began her course of study at Nahalal. She worked with chickens, cleaned cow sheds, and ploughed the fields. She delighted in sending her mother pictures of her life as a farmer, as she knew Catherine would be both amused and horrified by the sharp contrast between Hannah's cosmopolitan upbringing in Budapest and her new life in Palestine.

Hannah Senesh at Nahalal Agricultural School for Girls.

Despite her commitment to agriculture and *kibbutz** life, Hannah had second thoughts about her chosen path. In a letter to her brother Giora *(see in the longer film)*, she writes: "I want to be honest. This work doesn't have just a romantic side. When I hoe, or clean something, or wash dishes, or scatter the manure, I must confess the thought strikes me at times that I could be putting my abilities to better use. I'm fine, but I really miss you and Mother."

In 1941, Hannah completed her education at Nahalal and moved to a kibbutz. Although she could have gone to an established kibbutz founded by Hungarian speakers who knew her and admired her father, Hannah chose a more difficult path. She picked Kibbutz Sdot-Yam, a new settlement near Ceasarea. The kibbutz was merely a group of tents on the sand. Here Hannah became even more conflicted about the contrast between her dreams of becoming a writer and the realities of daily life on a kibbutz. In January 1942, Hannah confided in her diary, "I am tormented by grave doubts concerning my work. I stand on my feet nine hours daily, washing clothes. And I ask myself, is this my purpose in life?"

During this time, Hannah became increasingly concerned about the safety of her mother in Budapest and her brother in France. She also struggled to fit in with the mostly young "Sabras" (Israeli born) members of the kibbutz—the majority of whom had not had anything like the European culture and education that Hannah had received. Hannah's nephew Eitan Senesh explains, "She couldn't share anything with anyone at the kibbutz. She didn't have a friend, a boyfriend or something. She had no one here close, really close to her." According to Eitan Senesh, this profound loneliness had a central impact on Hannah's fateful life decisions to come.

In late 1942, news reached Palestine from Europe about the systematic mass killings of Jews by the Nazis. Hannah tried to obtain visas or arrange clandestine ways for her mother and her brother to come to Palestine. Hannah knew her mother would resist leaving Hungary. She sent a letter to her through secret channels: "Darling Mother. At the moment there is a real possibility for you to come and join me. I know that this is very sudden, but you must not hesitate. Every day is precious now."

But Catherine was unable to obtain a visa to leave Hungary. In addition, in late 1942, Germany invaded previously free Vichy France, forcing Giora to flee over the Pyrenees to Spain. Catherine and Hannah lost track of Giora and had no idea if he was dead or alive.

It was in this personal context that, in 1943, Hannah decided to volunteer for a mission, sponsored by the British Army, to help rescue downed Allied pilots and to rescue Jews in Central Europe. Of 250 Palestinian Jews originally considered, 30–35 were chosen for the mission, just three of them being women. Hannah's unit would go to Hungary. Hannah went to a British parachute school in Palestine.

---

*A *kibbutz* is a collective community in Israel, which historically was based on agriculture, that combines communal living, socialism, and Zionism.

In early 1944, the day before she was to leave for Cairo to complete her training, Hannah learned that her brother Giora had made it safely to Palestine by boat from Spain. They spent one day and night together before she left, yet Hannah didn't tell Giora anything about the mission she was about to embark on.

On March 14, 1944, Hannah parachuted behind enemy lines into Yugoslavia where she and the other paratroopers connected with partisans who would assist in the mission. Unfortunately, the group landed just days before the Germans occupied Hungary. The German invasion made the mission as planned impossible, but Hannah insisted on crossing the border into Hungary anyway.

Hannah and her brother the day before she leaves for her mission.

Hannah entered Hungary by crossing a river along with three resistance fighters. They agreed to help Hannah transport her British radio across the river. One of the men put Hannah's radio headset in his pocket. In a border village, the young man with the headphones was caught by Hungarian gendarmes. Inexplicably, he pulled out a pistol and killed himself. His suicide alerted the police that something was amiss, and when the area was searched, Hannah was discovered hiding on the outskirts of the village. She was tortured for her radio code before being sent to Budapest.

In a Gestapo prison in Budapest, Hannah and her mother Catherine were reunited for the first time in five years in an interrogation room. When Catherine did not agree to force Hannah to give the Germans her radio code, Catherine was arrested. Catherine and Hannah spent three months in the same prison in the summer of 1944, communicating across the courtyard from their windows and occasionally meeting in secret. In September 1944, Catherine was released and tried to save her daughter, braving the streets of Budapest at a time of chaos and deadly violence against Jewish people. Despite Catherine's desperate efforts, Hannah Senesh was executed for treason against Hungary on November 7, 1944.

HISTORICAL TIMELINE

In the following timeline, the shaded points refer specifically to Hungary and to the life of Hannah Senesh.

1921
Hannah is born July 17, Budapest, Hungary. Her brother Giora is one year her senior.

1927
Hannah's father, Bela Senesh, dies of a heart attack.

1933
The Nazi Party wins power in Germany after gaining the most votes in parliamentary elections. Adolf Hitler becomes chancellor, or prime minister, of Germany.

The Nazis "temporarily" suspend civil liberties for all citizens. Those liberties are never restored.

1934
At the age of 13, Hannah begins to write in her diary.

Hitler combines the positions of chancellor and president to become "Führer," or leader, of Germany.

1935
Germany's Nuremberg Laws deprive Jews of citizenship and other fundamental rights.

The Nazis intensify the persecution of political dissidents and others considered "racially inferior," including gypsies, Jehovah's Witnesses, and homosexuals. Many are sent to concentration camps.

1937
Hannah's grandmother Fini Mama dies.

1938
On Kristallnacht, the night of November 9–10, Nazi gangs attack Jews throughout Germany and Austria: 30,000 Jews are arrested, 91 are killed. Thousands of Jewish-owned shops and businesses are looted and more than 1,000 synagogues are set on fire.

At the age of 17, Senesh writes the poem "Now."

Giora Senesh leaves for France.

Hannah announces in her diary, "I've become a Zionist."

1939
In March, Germany takes over Czechoslovakia.

On September 1, Germany invades Poland.

In September Hannah leaves Hungary for Palestine. With her two children gone, Catherine Senesh is now alone in Budapest.

On September 19 Hannah arrives in Haifa, Palestine.

On September 23 Hannah arrives at the Nahalal Agricultural School for Girls in Palestine.

World War II begins as Britain and France declare war on Germany.

Jews are required to wear armbands or yellow stars.

1940

The Nazis begin deporting German Jews to Poland. Jews are forced into ghettos.

Germany conquers the Netherlands, Denmark, Norway, Belgium, Luxembourg, and France.

The Nazis begin the first mass murders of Jews in Poland.

1941

Germany attacks the Soviet Union.

October–November, Operation Reinhard begins with the construction of killing centers at Chelmno, Sobibor, Belzec, and Treblinka.

In two days, mobile killing units (*Einsatzgruppen*) shoot 33,771 Ukrainian Jews at Babi Yar—the largest single massacre of the Holocaust. *Einsatzgruppen* begin the systematic slaughter of Jews.

After the Japanese bomb Pearl Harbor, Germany—an ally of Japan—declares war on the United States.

Hannah graduates agriculture school and joins Kibbutz Sdot-Yam.

1942

At the Wannsee Conference, Nazi officials turn over the "Final Solution"—their plan to kill all European Jews—to the government.

Five death camps begin operation: Majdanek, Sobibor, Treblinka, Belzec, and Auschwitz-Birkenau.

The ghettos of Eastern Europe are emptied as thousands of Jews are deported to death camps.

By March, 20 percent to 25 percent of the Jews who would die in the Holocaust have already been murdered.

Allied radio broadcasts acknowledge that the Germans are systematically murdering the Jews of Europe.

As the Germans occupy Vichy France, Giora Senesh is forced to flee to Spain over the Pyrenees. Catherine and Hannah lose contact with him.

At the age of 21, Senesh writes the poems "At the Crossroads" and "Walk to Caesarea (Eli Eli)."

1943

By February, 80 percent to 85 percent of the Jews who would die in the Holocaust have been murdered.

Determined to return to Hungary, Hannah joins a top-secret rescue mission. Between 30 and 35 Palestinian Jews are chosen for the mission from a pool of 250. Hannah is one of three women chosen.

Hannah trains at a British parachute school near Haifa.

1944

In January Giora makes it to Palestine from Spain. He and Hannah spend one day together before Hannah leaves Palestine for Cairo to complete her training for the mission to rescue Jews from Hungary.

On March 14 Hannah parachutes into Yugoslavia to join with partisan groups who will help smuggle them across the border into Hungary. (See section called Partisan Movements in this guide for more information.)

On March 19 Hitler takes over Hungary and, despite the increasing possibility of defeat, begins deporting 12,000 Jews each day to Auschwitz, where they are murdered.

Between May 15 and July 8, 437,402 Hungarian Jews are put on trains and deported. Most are sent to Auschwitz, where they are murdered.

On June 6, D-Day, the Allied invasion of Western Europe begins.

At the age of 22, Hannah writes, "Blessed Is the Match" and "We Gather Flowers."

On June 9, Hannah and three resistance fighters cross into Hungary from Yugoslavia. Hannah is captured just after crossing the border.

Hannah is transferred for interrogation to the Gestapo barracks in Budapest.

On June 17, Catherine is summoned to the same barracks for questioning. She is reunited with Hannah in a Nazi interrogation room. Catherine is arrested and put in the same prison as Hannah.

Shortly before turning 23 Hannah writes her final poem "One-Two-Three."

In July, Soviet forces liberate Vilna, Lithuania.

Hannah communicates with her mother and other prisoners from her cell window.

In September, Hannah is placed in a cell next to Catherine's. Later that month, Catherine is released.

On October 15, just as Admiral Horthy, the Hungarian leader, is about to make peace with the Allies, the Arrow Cross regime, an antisemitic, fascist party modeled after the Nazis, overthrows the government.

On October 28 Hannah is tried for treason against Hungary in a military court. The judges postpone giving a verdict.

On November 7 Hannah is convicted of treason, sentenced to death, and executed. This was later determined to be judicial murder—as no sentence was ever officially given in the case.

1945

By April 1945 Soviet troops have liberated all of Hungary from the Nazis and the Arrow Cross.

World War II ends in Europe; the Holocaust is over; one-third of the world's Jews have been murdered.

The death camps are emptied.

By the end of 1945, Catherine arrives in Palestine.

1946

An International Military Tribunal in Nuremberg is created by Britain, France, the United States, and the Soviet Union. At Nuremberg, Nazi leaders are tried for war crimes and crimes against humanity.

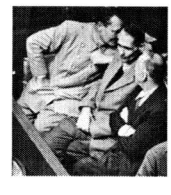

1948

On May 14 Israel is declared an independent state by the United Nations.

1950

Hannah's remains are moved by the state of Israel from the Jewish cemetery in Budapest to the national cemetery in Jerusalem.

1992

Catherine Senesh passes away at the age of 96.

1995

Giora Senesh passes away at the age of 76.

Additional Resources:

The Hannah Senesh Legacy Foundation, *www.hannahsenesh.org.il*

Film website: *www.blessedisthematch.com*

Hannah Senesh, *Hannah Senesh: Her Life and Diary*, the First Complete Edition, (Jewish Lights Publishing, 2004). http://jewishlights.com/

Peter Hay, *Ordinary Heroes: The Life and Death of Chana Szenes, Israel's National Heroine* (Athena, 1989).

CLASSROOM STRATEGIES

Finding One's Voice

In the film *Blessed Is the Match*, some of the most important and meaningful ways the viewer learns about Senesh and her life is through her own words. Throughout the film, excerpts from Senesh's diaries and letters to her family as well as her poems are woven into the telling of the story.

Senesh began keeping a diary when she was 13 years old. The diary excerpts used in the film provide the viewer with private details of her life, her thoughts, and her motivations, which would have remained unknown without her diary entries. The letters that Senesh wrote to her brother after he left Hungary for the presumed safety of France, as well as those that she wrote to her mother and brother after arriving in Palestine, also offer an important window into her life experiences.

- If students keep a personal journal or diary, ask them to reflect on why they write. If they don't keep a journal, ask students to think about why a person might be motivated to keep a diary.

- What information might a person choose to record in a diary?

- How might this be similar to or different from what a person would record in a letter to a family member? Would a letter that you write to a close friend be different from one you would write to a parent or sibling?

Senesh began writing poetry at age 6 after the death of her father. She continued to write poetry throughout her life, even managing to compose poems while imprisoned in the Gestapo barracks in Budapest after she was captured.

- How is writing a poem similar to or different from keeping a journal or writing letters? Are there different motivations? Are there different purposes?

One of the main themes of the film is Senesh's evolution as a poet and as an artist. Ask students to think of a musician or writer whose lyrics or writing they find inspirational. Ask them to respond in their journals to the following questions related to the artist they chose.

- Why do you find this artist's lyrics meaningful?

- Can you think of one line in a song that is particularly inspirational?

- How does the writer or artist use words or imagery to convey the meaning of the song?

- Do you know something about the artist's life that you think influences his or her music?

- How does a person develop his or her skills to become an inspirational artist?

Invite students to share their responses to these questions with a partner.

Senesh often reflected in her diary about developing the skills to become a talented writer. Aharon Megged, who is featured in the film *Blessed Is the Match,* met Senesh when she moved to Palestine. When he met Hannah, Megged was already a respected writer in the country. He tells the following story.

> One winter evening during the rain, she came to me with a notebook and she said these are my poems. The next day I told her, this is beautiful, but you are too influenced by another poet who was well known in those days. . . . She took this to heart. Two or three weeks later, Hannah brought more poetry. This was much better and more individual. She had found her voice.

In response to the previous quote, ask students to reflect on the following questions. What does it mean to have found one's voice? Think about your own writing. Are there times when you feel that you have really found your own voice? Thinking back to the artist you wrote about, would you say he or she has found his or her voice? Can you think of a point in the artist's career that you would say exemplifies that artist finding his or her voice?

Ask students to think, as they watch the film, about what life experiences contributed to Senesh finding her voice through her poetry.

Reviewing the Message from the Film Director
Ask students to read the Message from the Director, on page V of this guide.

- What were Grossman's motivations in making this film? How has her interest in Senesh evolved and changed through the years?

Defining a Hero
Introduce Senesh using the background information provided in this guide. This introduction does not need to be exhaustive, as students will learn more about Senesh as they watch the film.

In the message written for this study guide by the director, Grossman explains that Senesh is a national heroine in Israel. Who would you consider to be a national hero for your country? Why do you think this person is a national hero? What qualities does this person possess? Why do you think countries have national heroes?

Magda Creosy, a classmate of Senesh's in Budapest, says the following about Senesh: "I don't really like when they overuse the expression *hero*. I think there are very few real heroes, and she is one of them. Hannah is one of the real heroes."

Why do you think Creosy feels that people overuse the word *hero*? Ask students to think of a person who they believe would qualify as "one of the real heroes." Ask students to write in their journals about what makes this person a hero and to list five heroic qualities this person possesses.

Compile a list of all the heroic qualities from the students. Ask students to use this list to create a working definition of the word hero. You will return to this definition after the students watch the film.

Postview

After watching the film with your class, allow time for students to quietly reflect in their journals. Students might choose to write about moments from the film that resonated with them, questions that remained unanswered, thoughts about some of the main themes of the film, or simply their impression of the film.

CLASSROOM STRATEGIES

Identity, Decision Making, and Voice

Students can draw an identity chart to graphically convey aspects of a person's identity. Qualities that can be included in an identity chart are personality traits; memberships in different groups; hobbies and interests; and relationships with family, friends, and community. Students should also include in the chart the external influences that are impacting the person's identity. Following are examples of an identity chart:

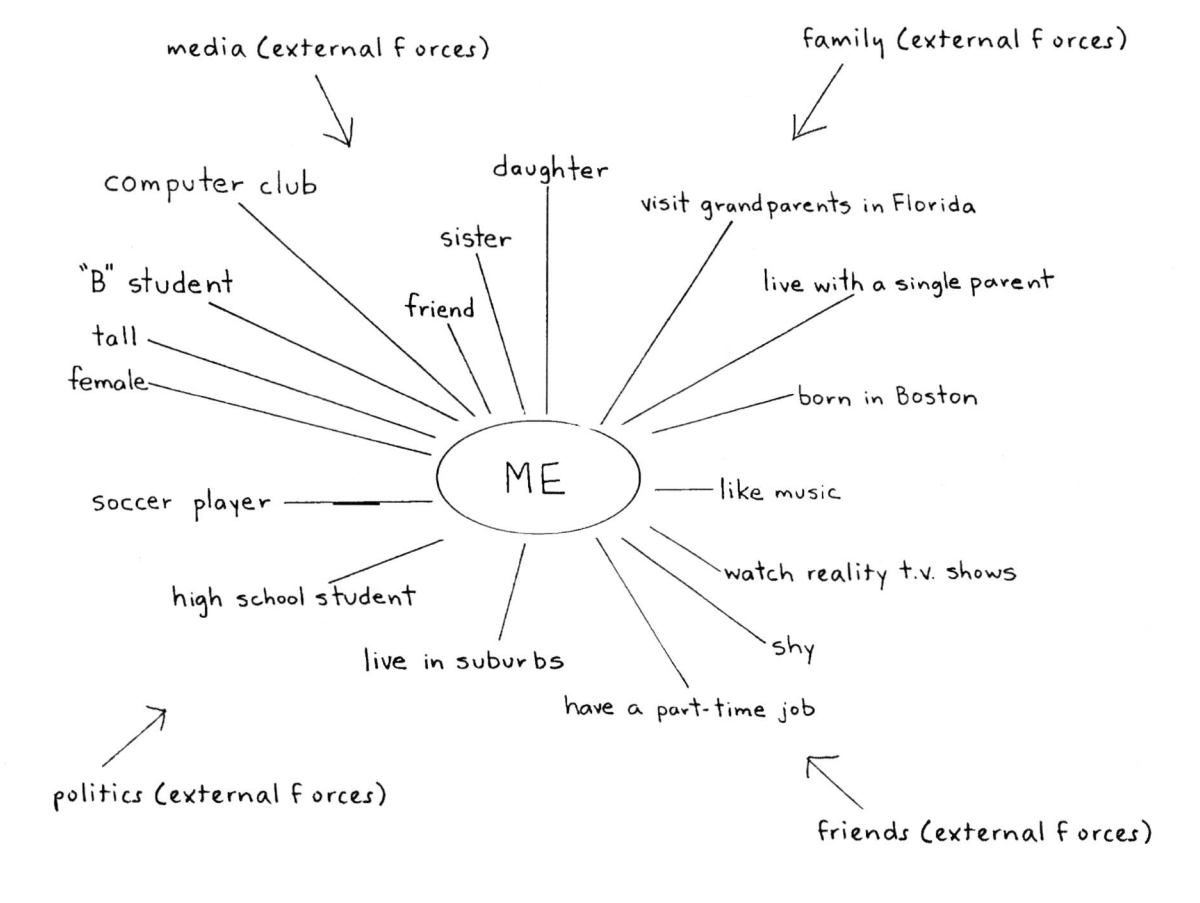

[Identity chart centered on "ME" with the following attributes radiating outward: media (external forces), family (external forces), computer club, daughter, sister, visit grandparents in Florida, "B" student, friend, live with a single parent, tall, female, born in Boston, soccer player, like music, high school student, watch reality t.v. shows, live in suburbs, shy, have a part-time job, politics (external forces), friends (external forces)]

After students watch the film, divide the class into small groups (there should be at least three groups) and assign each group one of the following periods in Hannah's life:

1. Adolescence in Hungary

2. Life in Palestine (Students may want to focus on Hannah's time studying at Nahalal or living on Kibbutz Sdot-Yam.)

3. After her decision to join the rescue mission to return to Hungary

Each group should create an identity chart for Senesh, reflecting the assigned period in her life. The external influences might include the environment in which Senesh lived, including her relationship to her family and Hungarian and European politics. For additional details students can also refer to the information on Senesh's life found in the Preview (both in the description of her life, as well as in the introduction from Hannah's family) section of this guide. Ask each group to share the identity chart they created.

Ask students to examine the identity charts from the three different periods and respond to the following questions:

· What qualities or characteristics are constant and can be seen in each chart?

· What has changed?

· How do the qualities or characteristics in each stage influence and impact Senesh's actions and the choices that she makes in each period of her life? By examining the identity charts from the different periods, do you have any insight into why Hannah chose to leave her home and go to Palestine, chose to study agriculture and later move to Sdot-Yam, and eventually join the rescue mission to Hungary?

Ask students to think of two significant moments in their lives, and create an identity chart for both of these periods. Students can share their identity charts in pairs and discuss the same three questions they considered in relation to the charts they created for Senesh:

· What qualities or characteristics are constant and can be seen in each chart?

· What has changed?

· How do the qualities or characteristics in each stage influence and impact your actions and the choices you made in both periods reflected in your identity charts?

Analyzing Poetry

As with other poets, Senesh's writing was deeply influenced by her life circumstances at the time she composed her poetry. The following three poems were written at each of the stages of her life.

1. Adolescence in Hungary: "Now," 1938, Tatra, Biela Voda (a vacation location that Hannah visited with her cousin in the summer of 1938)

2. Life in Palestine: "At the Crossroads," 1942, Caesarea

3. After the decision to join the rescue mission to return to Hungary: "Blessed Is the Match," May 2, 1944, Sardice, Yugoslavia

Divide students into three groups to examine one of the three poems found in the Handout section of the guide. Each student should first reflect on the meaning of the poem on his or her own. Then ask students to respond to the following questions in their journals. Once students have had time to reflect on the poem ask them to share their responses with the other students who studied the poem. Each group should then share a summary of the group members' conversation with the whole class.

- How is the poem influenced by the personal circumstance of Senesh's life at the time she composed the poem?
- How might the situation in Europe at the time have impacted the poem? Students can look at the Historical Timeline to assist with answering this question.

Conclude this part of the lesson by asking the following question: How do these poems demonstrate Senesh's growth as a person and as a writer?

From a literary perspective each poem demonstrates Senesh's increased sophistication as a writer. She becomes more skilled in her use of imagery, voice, and repetition. You may want to ask your students to examine each poem through this lens, looking at her use of literary tools such as those listed above as well as tone, personification, and metaphor.

Thinking back to one of the moments for which the students drew a personal identity chart, ask students to compose a poem (you may also decide to give the option of a visual art portrayal) that is a reflection and an expression of this time in their lives.

If you have time you may want to organize a poetry reading in which students can share the poems they wrote.

You may also ask students to re-read each of Senesh's poems from this section and ask students to choose one poem they find particularly meaningful. You can ask students why they chose the poem. Is there a line from the poem that specifically resonates for him/her?

Return to the Concept of a Hero
Looking back at the working definition of the term *hero* that the class developed before watching the film, do they think Hannah's character and actions fit this definition? After watching the film are there other characteristics or qualities of a hero that students might add to the definition? Would they want to adapt or amend their working definition of a hero? You may want to share the dictionary definition of "hero," **noun** (pl. *heroes*) a person, typically a man, who is admired for their courage or outstanding achievements. What else would you add?

As a six-year-old in Budapest, Hungary, Ervin Staub was first hidden to protect him from the Nazis, and then he and other family members survived with the protective passes Raoul Wallenberg and other embassies in Budapest created. (For more information on Wallenberg, see the "International Response to the Holocaust" in the Research Project section of this guide.) When Staub grew up he became a psychologist who studied the roots of evil as well as what motivated people to do good. He concludes, "Goodness, like evil, often begins in small steps. Heroes evolve; they aren't born."[2]

Ask students to respond in their journals to how this quote might relate to Senesh's life.

Rescue and Responsibility

In 1944, when she was living in Palestine, Senesh joined a rescue mission to return to Hungary as a paratrooper. She understood the risks involved in such a mission and yet she still chose to participate. Ask students to reflect on moments from the film and respond in their journals to the question of why Senesh made the decision to risk her life and go back into Hungary.

In the Handout section of this guide, you will find selected quotations taken from the feature-length version of *Blessed Is the Match*. The quotes reflect each individual responding in his or her own way to the question of why this group of Jewish young people signed up for the rescue mission. Students should read each quote and choose lines or words that resonate with them or choose sections of text that relate to the question of motivation and responsibility—or do both.

Ask students to create a poem, often called a Found Poem, with the lines that resonated for them. Students each pick three quotations and work in small groups to organize all of the words and sentences into a poem that respond to the question of why the young people chose to join the mission to parachute back into Europe. You can also have students work independently. In this case each student would choose five to 10 quotations or words and create his or her own Found Poem.

Ask students to choose a title for their poems and write a short paragraph about the meaning of the title and why it is appropriate for the poems they composed.

Invite the students to share their poems with the whole class, in small groups, or in pairs. Conclude the lesson by reading the following poem written by Senesh in 1944 after she joined the rescue mission.

"We Gather Flowers" (1944)

We gathered flowers in the fields and mountains,
We breathed the fresh winds of spring,
We were drenched with the warmth of the sun's rays
In our Homeland, in our beloved home.

We go out to our brothers, in exile,
To the suffering of winter, to frost in the night.
Our hearts will bring tidings of springtime,
Our lips sing the song of light.

You can choose whether you ask students to interpret the poem or simply end the class with Senesh's voice, through the reading of her poem.

Research Projects
The following two topics for student research, "Partisan Groups during World War II" and "International Response to the Holocaust," provide additional context for the historical period students learned about in *Blessed Is the Match*.

Partisan Groups during World War II
Senesh and the brigade of Jewish paratroopers from Palestine met up with partisan groups once they landed in Yugoslavia. A partisan is "a member of an organized body of fighters who attack or harass an enemy, especially within occupied territory; a guerrilla." There were two very active partisan groups in Yugoslavia at the time of the mission from Palestine.

Students can collect information on partisan groups during World War II and present their findings to the class. This could be an oral presentation, a PowerPoint, or an essay.

For information on partisan groups, as well as lessons and resources on the topic, visit *www.jewishpartisans.org*.

International Response to the Holocaust
At the beginning of the film we learn that the mission of Jewish paratroopers from Palestine was the only military rescue mission for Jews during World War II.

Students can investigate various aspects of international responses to the Holocaust. The following topics highlight both the inadequate reaction of Allied countries, as well as heroic responses by certain international diplomats who saved Jews during the Holocaust.

- The Evian Conference: Students can learn about the international conference convened by U.S. President Franklin D. Roosevelt in July 1938. Delegates representing 32 countries gathered to discuss the fate of the Jews in Nazi-controlled Germany and Austria.

- Immigration: Students can investigate the World War II immigration policy of the country in which they reside. Were Jews given permission to enter the country? How many were permitted entry? What years was immigration permitted? What influenced the immigration policy?

- Diplomats and Visas: Students can learn about diplomats such as Wallenberg and Sempo Sugihara, who provided Jews with visas for Sweden and Japan, respectively, that ultimately saved thousands of Jews. Wallenberg, a Swedish diplomat, is a particularly appropriate research topic, as he saved thousands of Hungarian Jews by creating safe houses and providing visas for the Jews of Budapest.

Endnotes:
1. Hannah Senesh, *Hannah Senesh: Her Life and Diary*, the First Complete Edition, Paperback (Jewish Lights Publishing, 2004), xxix.

2. Daniel Goleman, "Great Altruists: Science Ponders Soul of Goodness" *The New York Times*, March 5, 1985
http://query.nytimes.com/gst/fullpage.html?res=9C03EFD81039F936A35750C0A963948260&sec= health&spon=&pagewanted=3 (accessed on April 22, 2008).

HANDOUT ONE

POETRY BY HANNAH SENESH: Identity, Decision Making, and Voice

"Now" (1938)

Now—now I'd like to say something,
Something more than mere words,
More dappled than color,
More musical than rhythm or rhyme,
Something a million people haven't already said or heard.

Just something.
All about the land is silent, listening,
The forest gazing at me, expectant.
The sky watches me with a curious eye.
Everything is silent. And so am I.

"At the Crossroads" (1942)

A voice called. I went.
I went for it called.
I went lest I fall.
At the crossroads,
I blocked both ears with white frost.
And cried for what I had lost.

"Blessed Is the Match" (1944)

Blessed is the match consumed in kindling flame
Blessed is the flame that burns in the secret fastness of the heart
Blessed is the heart with strength to stop its beating for honor's sake
Blessed is the match consumed in kindling flame.

HANDOUT TWO

RESCUE AND RESPONSIBILITY

"We wanted to caress the shoulder of the Jew and tell them we came to bring you regards and to help you from Eretz Israel (Palestine)."
—Surika Braverman

"It's extremely difficult to send somebody else to such a mission. Your first reaction is let me go. On the other hand I knew many of them personally. They didn't wait to be sent. They volunteered."
—Shimon Peres

"It is easy to say it was a suicide mission. What if it was? What if it was? What's wrong with trying to save people in danger?"
—Reuven Darfni (01:07:30; lower thirds: Parachutist Reuven Dafni, Final Interview, 2005)

"And when she was asked, Hannah, why do you go on a mission? She said, in my heart, there are two great loves. One love is of my nation, my people. And my second love is my mother."
—Surika Braverman

"December 26, 1943. Darling Giora: I am starting something new. Perhaps it's madness. Perhaps it's fantastic. Perhaps it is dangerous. . . . I wonder, will you understand? Will you believe that it is more than a childish wish for adventure, more than youthful romanticism that attracted me? There are times when one is commanded to do something, even at the price of one's life."
—Hannah Senesh

ABOUT THE PARTNERSHIP

In the spirit of Hannah's courage and as a means to bring her story to the widest possible audience, Katahdin Productions is engaging in a national outreach campaign to accompany the documentary feature *Blessed Is the Match: The Life and Death of Hannah Senesh* (*www.blessedisthematch.com*). Katahdin Productions is a nonprofit production company dedicated to creating high-quality documentary films, educational materials, and media outreach projects that open minds, provoke dialogue and encourage positive social change. Katahdin has partnered with Facing History and Ourselves to fulfill the educational initiative part of their outreach campaign. Facing History has helped to create a classroom DVD version of *Blessed Is the Match: The Life and Death of Hannah Senesh* and has created supplemental materials to accompany the DVD for dissemination in seminars and workshops around the country. For more information, visit *www.facinghistory.org* to access the educational materials and *www.katahdin.org* for more resources or information about the film.